Linda Giacomino

SOUL *Pretty*

Visual Story Design and Text Copyright © 2019 by Linda Giacomino

Illustrations Copyright © 2019 by Paula Romani

All Rights Reserved. No part of this publication may be reproduced, stored in a retrieval system or transmitted in any form by any means electronic, mechanical, or photocopying, recording or otherwise without the permission of the author.

For more information, please contact:
Mascot Books
620 Herndon Parkway #320
Herndon, VA 20170
info@mascotbooks.com

Library of Congress Control Number: 2014922022

CPSIA Code: PRTWP0319A
ISBN-13: 9780986340000

Printed in Malaysia

Francesca & Hyla ~ your light has brightened my life.
It's because of you.

SOUL *Pretty*

A girl's journey toward self-discovery

LINDA GIACOMINO

illustrated by

PAULA ROMANI

Start the day with a smile
and let your **inner beauty** shine.
Believe in yourself and know **you can**
achieve anything **you** put your mind to.

See the **good** in everyone
and the **bright** side of everything.
Remember to **treat others** the way
you want to be treated, and **always** find
the strength to follow your **own path**.

Come along for a ride,
just **you** and **me**,

to see how **pretty**
our **souls** can be.

FAITH

It's all about believing.
You don't know how it will happen,
but you know it will.

HONESTY

Others might not know you told the truth, but you always will. When you're honest, you never have to keep your story straight.

but life's experiences will make you wise.

SELF-ACCEPTANCE

Accepting yourself for who you are will give you *inner peace*, and it will show by the twinkle in your eyes and the sparkle in your smile.

LOVE

It's when you care so much
your heart feels a special way;
this feeling gets more and more
amazing each and every day.

Life is like a painting.

Choose your colors extra wise and you'll create a masterpiece.

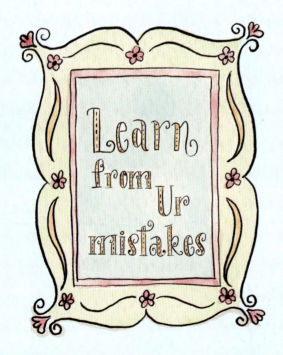

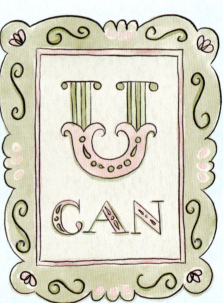

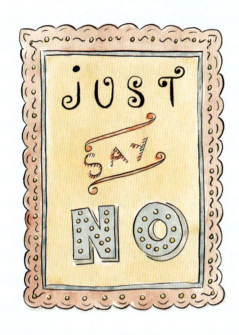

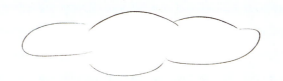
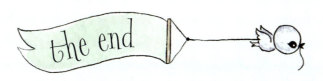
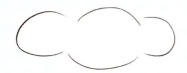
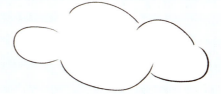